From Call to Client

The Official Guide To Hypnotic Phone Consultations

That Convert Prospects Into

High Paying and Satisfied

Quit Smoking Clients

By Jess Marion and Shawn Carson and Sarah Carson

From Call to Client: The Official Guide to Hypnotic Phone Consultations That Convert Prospects Into High Paying and Satisfied Quit Smoking Clients

Copyright 2015 Jess Marion, Shawn Carson, Sarah Carson and Changing Mind Publishing. All rights reserved

All images produced with www.easel.ly.com

No part of this book may be reproduced in any manner whatsoever without written permission except in the case of brief quotations embedded in critical articles and reviews.

For further information please contact Changing Mind Publishing at 545 8th Avenue, Suite 930, New York, N.Y. 10018

Is this Phone Conversation Familiar?

YOU ARE NOT ALONE

Prospective clients do not know how to value a hypnosis service. They do not know much about our field and in many cases are even a little afraid to call at first. The only means they have of choosing a hypnotist is by price.

If they are new to hypnosis they can only rely on price and while they may be willing to pay thousands of dollars to a traditional therapist they are more reluctant to spend that kind of money with a hypnotist

It is your job to show them your value and get them in touch with how important the change is to them.

Prospective clients need you to make it easy for them to choose to work with you. Your job when a prospect calls is to decide if you are a good match for them and if so to make the sales process comfortable.

Phone conversations are inherently hypnotic They require fixated attention, catalepsy, and elicit unconscious responses. Don't believe me? Next time you are on the phone switch ears at some point and feel what happens.

The cool thing is your prospects will be in a trance when they call. Why not use hypnosis to sell hypnosis?

Ethics for Hypnotic Selling

1 Our goal is not manipulate people but to make the sales process easier. To do this want the best for your prospect. Don't want anything from them. Hypnotic selling creates a Win-Win relationship.

2 Never promise what you cannot deliver. Understand the limits of your skills and refer on when necessary. Also, always over deliver. This is good for your clients and good for business.

3 Using hypnosis to sell unethically leads to buyer's remorse for the client and a poor reputation for the hypnotist. If you get a sense that the prospect will not benefit from your services feel comfortable being honest with them. If you don't believe they can change with you then do NOT continue the sales process..

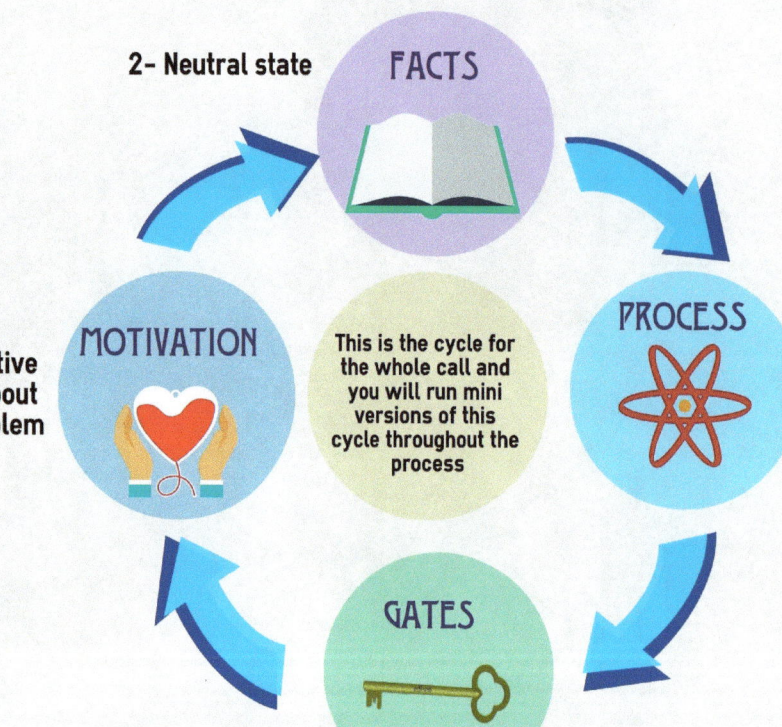

"What do you want to accomplish with hypnosis?"

Motivation GATES

1 Is their motivation to change toward a goal or away from something they don't want?

If toward results you can covertly remind them that they don't have the result yet. The first step is for the prospect to be away from a problem.

If away from what they don't want you will transition them toward positive results soon.

You need to associate them into the pain of the problem before moving on to the things they want. This works with how the brain is setup

"Tell me about the last time you had this. How is this a problem for you?"

2 and 3

It is less important what they are saying than how they are feeling. You should hear state changes.
Emotions drive this process so build up states.

"Why do you want to change now?"

4 Does their motivation come from them or is it because others want them to change?

If the change is mainly from others is: the doctor or spouse wants it then the prospect's journey ends here. It is the others in their life that have the problem, not the prospect.

If the prospect wants the change for herself then she is in the right place to change. She has passed through this gate.

Studies show that intrinsic motivation is more effective than extrinsic motivation

5 and 6

> How do you want to be different? When you have been this way for a year, how are you being as a person?

Are the answers given stated in the positive?
We are not interested in what they don't want. We are deeply curious about how the prospect wants to be.

If answers are about what the prospect doesn't want we need to shift that response to the positive by letting them know we aren't interested in what they don't want but what they do want. You can be playful with this.

If positively stated then listen in for Hot Words. These are words from the prospect that are filled with emotion.

Hot words are unconsciously emphasized. They are anchors to strong states. Collect these from your prospect's responses to feed back to the prospect through out the call.

Section Tips

When a prospect asks for the fee at the start of the conversation do not give it to them. Say you will answer that in a moment but first you want to see if they are right for your program. This stops them from buying based on price.

Do not accept a new client based only on an email. Insist on speaking with them to make sure they are right for your program. This give the feeling of exclusivity. It also makes sure that you are a good fit for the prospect

Do not list your session prices on your website. You do not want clients buying based on price. It also avoids any issues if you refuse a prospect because they are not the right fit for you.

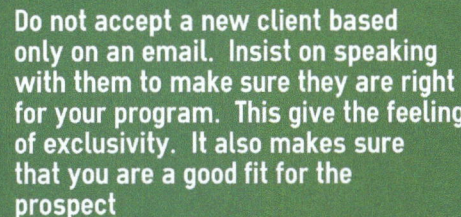
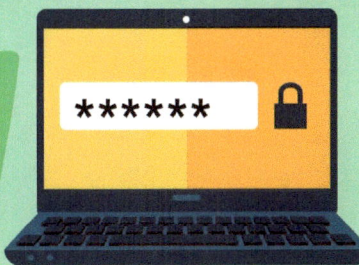

Just the Facts Please

| Giving facts about hypnosis builds certainty that hypnosis can help the prospect change. | Giving facts about neuroscience builds certainty that the process is based in reality and can help the prospect. | Giving your success rates builds certainty that you are experienced and the prospect could be successful with you. |

 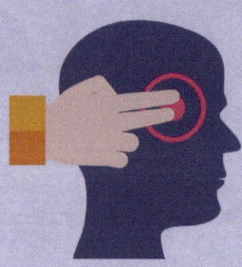 

Some Fun Facts

Giving facts creates a break state which is needed before the next step

- Brain scans show that hypnosis changes habits by changing the brain.
- Awesome! The conscious mind can only process 5-9 pieces of information at any time. The unconscious processes everything else in your experience.
- Did you know that people who quit smoking with hypnosis succeed 90% of the time?
- Wow thats high! Studies also show that hypnosis increases emotional wellbeing.

Process
The Art of the Processless

Prospects like a step by step process presented to them. It makes them confident that you are experienced with their issue and it gives them a sense of being able to chart out their progress.

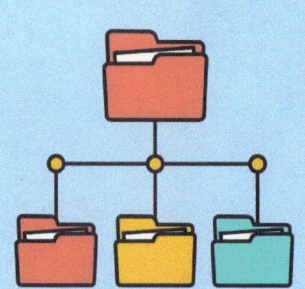

Because every client is different it is important to present a "process" that in reality is open ended but feels specific for the prospect. This is when you will begin to also use the prospect's Hot Words

All About States

- Use your process description as a chance to build up a strong positive state in the prospect

- By the end of this step the prospect should be feeling not only that they want to change but they are certain you're the one to help them achieve it.

- To help build the positive state use present tense languaging, hot words, and embedded commands.

Whatever state you want your prospect to feel you must feel first. Go first into good feelings and you will unconsciously communicate those feelings to your prospect.

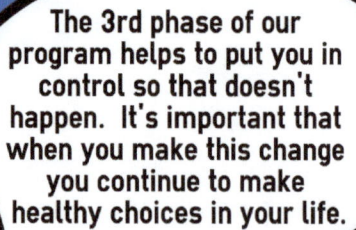

Section Tips

People like to hear about a process. This will automatically give you some level of authority.

The real goal of this portion of the phone conversation is to build a strong positive state for the prospect. Feed back the hot words they give and listen closely. You want to hear them consciously and unconsciously agreeing with you.

Take your time with this part and see how big of a positive state you can build by getting them in touch with what it will be like when they have achieved their goal.

The prospect's state and agreement is your gate for this portion of the conversation. Do not move on to the call to action- the "are you ready for the next step" until they have associated into a positive state.

The prospect needs to believe they can change and you are the one to help them get there.

THE FINAL GATES

While we want the prospect to feel good as they sign up we want to make sure they are not buying purely on a good state. This can lead to buyer's remorse, "no shows", and cancelations. We need to invite the conscious mind to the show.

This also ensures that the prospect is 100% committed to the change. Think of this as your last fail safe before taking on the client.

These gates will give the new client moments of success before coming in which will set the preframes for success in the session.

The Gates

Response to Price. If they agree move to next gate. If not you could offer a payment plan or not take them.

Offer Appointment Time. If they are inflexible with dates and times then you don't have compliance and will need to do some work during the session to get it.

Task Them. Have them smoke their last cigarette the night before and bring the pack with them. If they fight you on this they aren't ready to quit. Do not take them.

Add in any prerequisite for the session such as payment ahead of time or forms needing to be filled out.

Example

In the following section you will find an example of a typical phone consultation. You will also find some notes to guide you through the conversation. Enjoy!

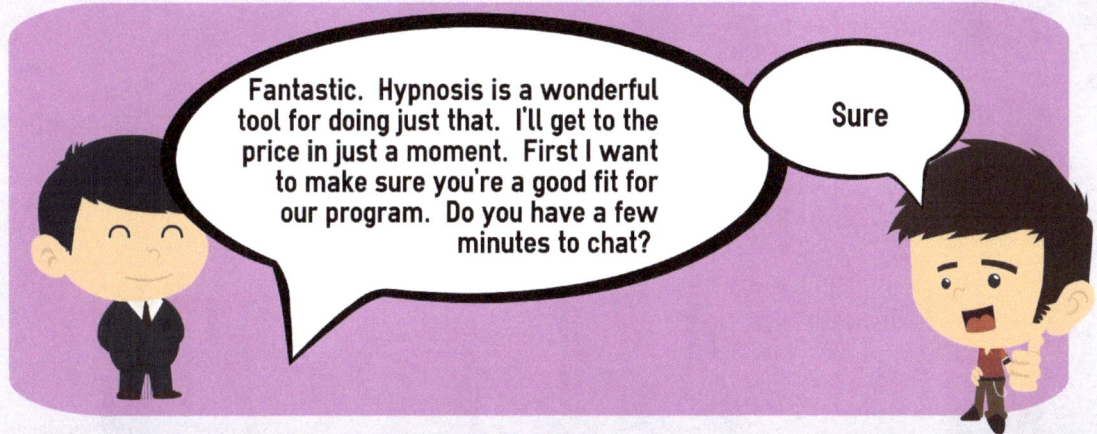

Our hypnotist does 3 important things in this section.

1- He acknowledges the price question and moves the prospect's attention away

2- When he says he wants to see if the prospect is a good fit for the program it gives the prospect the sense that there is a selective component to this and that he might not get to work with the hypnotists. This increases desire.

3- He asks if the prospect has time to chat. He is looking for agreement

"You said you smoked off and on, can you tell me a little about that?"

"Well I have tried to quit a number of times but went back either because something big happened or I started to snack too much"

"That is really common. I have worked with a number of people with similar experiences quitting with other methods"

This information will allow the hypnotist to out-frame the prospect's concern about failure. Whatever they did in the past the hypnotist will not do now.

This statement lets the prospect know that the hypnotist is experienced in the field. Notice the use of "other methods" this implies that their experience with hypnosis will be different.

"They say that hypnosis was the step they needed to quit for life. In fact I had a client a few months ago who was a 2 pack a day smoker who had tried to stop dozens of times. After his session he threw out his cigarettes. I ran into him a few days ago, he is still smoke free. You can succeed in quitting"

Client stories boost the prospect's confidence and tells the unconscious mind that the prospect can change too. Feel free to use embedded suggestions.

Only use true client stories.

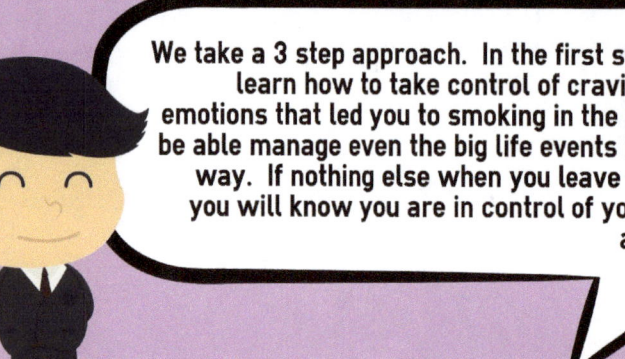

Notice that the hypnotist is tying in the information from the prospect to describe the process. He is speaking directly to the prospect's unconscious concern that they may go back to smoking when something big happens.

The prospect is also verbally agreeing which is an excellent sign that they are unconsciously invested in the hypnotist's message.

As the hypnotist is laying out the process he is closely listening to whether or not the prospect is stepping into good states. People buy based on emotions and only use logic to justify it later. The prospect should be getting more excited about coming to work with you.

During this process the hypnotist is addressing any experiences from the prospect's past that could be a block to their success.

www.ingramcontent.com/pod-product-compliance
Lightning Source LLC
LaVergne TN
LVHW072127070426
835512LV00002B/33